Secrets of the Fitness Industry

Weight-loss Without the Struggle!

CHANGED

WESLEY VIRGIN

Please feel free to send me an email. Just know that these emails are filtered by my publisher. Good news is always welcome.

Wesley Virgin - **wesley_virgin@awesomeauthors.org**

You might also want to check my blog for Updates and interesting info.
www.7dayfitness.com

About the Publisher

BLVNP Incorporated, A Nevada Corporation, 340 S. Lemon #6200, Walnut CA 91789, info@blvnp.com / legal@blvnp.com

CHANGED

**Secrets of the Fitness Industry
Weight-Loss without the Struggle**

By: Wesley Virgin

© **Wesley Virgin 2014**
ISBN: 978-1-68030-907-2

DEDICATION:

I dedicate this book to my two amazing children, Deasia and David. There were several times that they believed in me when I didn't believe in myself. I love you and thank you for making me a super happy dad!

WARNING!!!

What you are about to read is not intended to be skimmed, or skipped through. Please take your time and read EVERY SINGLE word very carefully, because I, MVT Wesley Virgin, am going to expose the secrets of the Health and Fitness industry, the secrets they do not want you to know about.

If you are well over the age of 30 and have tried all the late night infomercial fitness DVD's, read all the fitness and nutritional books, or have had the clipboard trainer and the unused gym memberships, with little to no results...

Then the strategies and techniques below are for you!!! It might just change your life! To be honest, if you read the entire book several times and apply everything daily—IT WILL!!

Let's Get Started!

TABLE OF CONTENTS

FOREWORD

It was a typical Wednesday. I woke up, had breakfast, wrote for a couple hours and then checked my email. Little did I know that in my inbox was an email that would strike up a friendship that I'm sure will last a lifetime.

To be honest, when I opened that email from Wesley Virgin, I almost didn't answer. But there was just something about the way he wrote that spoke to me and made me respond. After all, at one point I was in his very same position, scrambling to shout my message from the mountain tops to anyone who would listen.

Like the others before him, I put him to the test. He asked for my help in spreading his message of getting fit with passion, I asked for a few favors before I would consider helping. For most people, this scares them off and they crawl away with a sense of defeat thinking to themselves, "poor me, I'll never catch a break." Not Wesley!

To this day, he's the only person who asked for my help and then proceeded to follow the exact steps I laid out for him. Wesley Virgin is truly a man of his word and his slogan of getting fit with passion isn't just a catchy phrase he came up with, it's how he lives every second of his life!

It didn't take long for me to realize that Wesley Virgin knows the 2 special ingredients that it takes to succeed. Dedication and motivation!

He's clearly dedicated by the fact that he's helped thousands of people around the world get fit with passion which is no small feat for any one man. And as far as motivation goes, his self-styled title of "Master Motivator" cannot be more apt.

In fact, just the last time Wesley and I were on a call together, it felt like he was reaching through the screen and igniting me with his electric passion to motivate people that you can change the way you look, you can change the way you feel, you can change your energy levels, your attitude, your gratitude and sooo much more!

I'm grateful that Wesley emailed me that day and I'm glad I gave him a shot. Because I would have never known how intensely passionate someone could be about helping others without meeting him.

Give him the same chance I did and I promise you will not be disappointed!

- Tyler Bramlett
(the Garage Warrior)

INTRODUCTION

Before I begin, let me ask you a question. Do you recognize the guy in the pink shirt to my left in the pic below, maybe from a little show called Shark Tank? This is a funny but true story.

I caught Kevin Harrington, Shark Tank Superstar, while in Vegas at a Mastermind event, and literally tried to pitch him on my 7 Minute Blueprint while he was going to the bathroom! Bold, right?! LOL! But guess what happened? After pitching him at the toilet, he did not say the devastating words so many people hear on the show. "I AM OUT!!!" The multi-millionaire Kevin Harrington, who is the top dog in the SEEN ON TV niche and fitness industry, gave me some very encouraging words about 7DayFitness.

I was like WOW! Me, the owner of www.7DayFitness.com had the pleasure to mastermind with the star of Shark Tank, Kevin Harrington! He has an amazing business mind and is also a remarkable guy. It is amazing when folks who have a network of hundreds of millions, supports your business and idea, I am just waiting on his million-dollar-investment, LOL. But really, he is an awesome and amazing guy to meet.

So this book **"Changed: Secrets of the Fitness Industry, Weight-Loss without the Struggle,"** if used, will allow you to design, shape, tone and sculpt your body with more energy than you will know what to do with!!!

***

I am fortunate enough to run some very large bootcamps, maxing out at 100 Superstars (I hate the word clients) per night! And I was lucky enough to meet the CEO of the FIT BODY BOOTCAMP, probably one of the largest franchise bootcamps around the world.

I met Pedros, Ceo of FIT BODY BOOTCAMP, in Cali. He was not only interested in my unique concept but he supported me and wanted me to keep in contact with him to see how we could work together.

***

Now most of you might not recognize the guy in the picture below but have you ever heard of a program called, Truth About Abs? This is my friend Mike Geary who has one of the top six-pack ab programs, (second to mine of course lol) on the internet. He and I actually had a chance to meet in Vegas and had dinner at one the best steakhouses in the Palms Hotel.

I am not showing you all the pics to impress you or boast but I want to give you a sneak preview of who I am and the people that I associate with. Ok, let's jump into, and let me open up, a few secrets that are going wow you.

<u>Congratulations!</u>

Now let's talk about YOU!! Yes YOU, reading this right now. I would like to thank you and congratulate you for taking such massive action today.

By taking your finger and clicking on the "buy" button or picking up this book at your local book store, you are going to get a full access glimpse of powerful tips and tricks that celebs, body builders, and fitness models use to keep their physique beach body ready without a lot of effort. You are going to see how it feels to decrease your body fat percentage even if you have bad joints, a bad back or even a thyroid condition. You will also discover the all-natural products that men and women over the age of 30 should use to neutralize fat and toxins so the weight comes off even if you do not have time to work out.

I should know about the time factor. Hell!!... I have two kiddos. Sorry for all the pics of my children, but I love my munchkins dearly!! They are my REASONS WHY!! (I will explain the WHY concept later).

So if you are a soldier or soldierette that has been searching for the quickest and easiest way to accomplish great health, get tons of energy and a body that will cause the opposite sex to gravitate to you, you are reading the right book. Get ready to read every word very closely, because today you are going to get my personal EXACT strategies to LOSE, LEAN, TONE and SCULPT instantly without the discomfort or struggle! Sorry for the soldier and soldierette expression.

What can I say? I was in the Army for five years. LOL!

Why should I listen to Wes?

Sure I have been featured on the Dee Armstrong Show and Yahoo News!, and other national and international media networks around the world have labelled me as a World Authority in the Fitness Industry. But I have also instructed some of the largest bootcamps in Houston, TX, and I have already been contacted by many interested folks from around the world such as from Brazil, Canada, and the United Kingdom, who are currently using my system and achieving outrageous results because they are following the super simple, baby step advice from the cool army veteran you see below.

Look at that before and after picture. I have a funny story about how I joined the military that I will tell you about later. But one thing I would like to make CLEAR... Crystal Clear!! I don't BS at all!! Ever!! I may get a bit over excited in my videos (you can check out my free workouts at my blog www.7DayFitness.com/blog), and I may use a bit of foul language when I am speaking about the Food and Drug Administration, uneducated trainers and money grubbing gym facilities. But people like you should know the truth about what really works.

And one more thing before I peel off the label and expose the truth; don't let any doctor label you.

Label me? What do you mean, Wes?

Here are some of the statements I hear Superstars (I hate the word Clients) say after a doctor visit: You are obese! Your thyroid condition will keep you from losing weight! Take this pill and the fat will melt away! It is because of your genetics that you are fat!! Your metabolism will never speed up at your age! You will need fat loss surgery or Lipo. Your bone structure will prevent you from achieving the body you desire! You have to starve yourself skinny!

Really!!!! I call BS!!!!! I am going to share why, but first let me tell you who this handsome black guy is.

PREFACE

Before you set your eyes on the first page of the first chapter of this book, I would like you to know how much I thank you and appreciate you for entering what I call the 3%. I will talk more about this in the chapters ahead. But my name is Wesley Virgin and I am just a normal cool guy from Houston, Texas, father of 2 amazing children, a former Citrix engineer, who quit that industry to pursue a passion for helping others master their body without the struggle, around the world. From training so many wonderful superstars (I hate the word clients) and always exploring what works the best and what will give Superstars like yourself the best results faster, I finally decided to verbally vomit this information into a book.

Now let me be blunt, this book is not filled with boring stories and medical studies to cajole you into a certain way of thinking. No! In this short book I am going to give you the exact techniques and methods I use to look and feel like a 20-year-old, and I am almost 40!! I am going to show you how I am reversing the aging process easily without being fooled by the pills, drugs and late night quick fix infomercials. I am not sure what will happen to me once this book hits mainstream, because there are many people and companies out there who prefer I not publish this type of material. But guess what!! I don't care, I am going to express how I feel without the filter or holding back. And you deserve to know the freaking truth... I am an Outlier for life!! (Thanks Malcolm Gladwell, I will send you a link to his book later).

But you are going to see that I say whatever is on my mind to help the greater good, which is you, You are the greater good!! Here is a quick snapshot of my personal story.

I did not come from a rich family or a genetically fit family, and I never was the popular guy. I was the rebellious guy. As a matter of fact, my father and mother are pastors of a church here in Houston, TX. And if you know anything about PK kids, we are the most rebellious, baddest kids who can't wait to get out of our parents' house! I joined the military to get out of there! LOL! I love my dad but that guy was super strict and I HATED IT!!!

But I wasn't a popular kid in high school; I was that super skinny, shy and nerdy guy who didn't make good grades. Teachers couldn't stand me, because I was labeled as the class clown from grade 1. I think I would have made an amazing comedian like my boy Kevin Hart (GUY IS SUCH AN INSPIRATION), if I didn't jump into the fitness world. I still remember my favorite cousin, Shanta telling me, "Wesley you are such a character!" Basically I am the one in the family that did the outrageous crazy stuff, like jump out of planes, travel to Iraq by choice, drive a car with no lights, quit jobs without having a backup plan, file bankruptcy just to get a vehicle back from the mechanic, quit college because I thought it was stupid and a waste of my time, literally I could go on for days... LOL... But as you can see, I did not grow up with any special training or with a silver spoon in my mouth.

But to be transparent, I didn't like myself in the early years of my life. I hated my reflection in the mirror! My dad was too strict!! I didn't have any confidence to talk to the chicks! Friends around the neighborhood didn't like me! So in an attempt to be significant I started to live a life of rebellion, No Rules!! I didn't listen to anybody unless their name was Wesley Virgin IV. In short, I was a pretty unhappy dude for a big part of my early life. Hell!! I even tried to fight my Army Sergeant, which almost landed me in Army jail, when I found out he was banging the girl I was talking to at the time!!

But Question for you: Do you ever feel a certain type of way, when you look in the mirror late at night? You know when you self-reflect and think about life. It used to make me sad, depressed, angry and even disturbed at times, but no one even knew. I think we all feel this way at different stages in our life, but not many people have the guts to be vulnerable or share how they really feel. But I, Wesley Virgin, cool black guy from Houston, TX, is taking the first step today. I am putting it all out there to let you know it's ok. You know as human beings we always look for the flaws in our personal appearance, and we say crazy things to ourselves. I am Fat, I am Big, I am Skinny, I am not tall enough! My nose is too big! My lips aren't big enough! My belly looks disgusting! I hate my legs! I hate my hair! I hate my arms!!

And on and on and on... Instead of purposely searching for the beauty that our creator has blessed us with.

But to share some great news, things started to turn around for me when I started to master my body. I learned this from my unofficial mentor Tony Robbins. He says, "If you don't like something about yourself, CHANGE IT!" So I did. (**Note:** That statement applies to life as well.)

One thing you should know about me is that I am freakishly Passionate and I LOVE people, I love them for who they are, instead of what they do. There so many lies, misconceptions and parasitical people in the world. But guess what!! I am a real person!! This is my real body!! And I am writing this book!! I did not have the pleasure of having a ghost writer like other celebs, like DT...

Who is DT, Wes? Well let's just say I cannot say his name because he will sue my ass if I do... LOL! Let's just say DT is a shrewd business man who makes a lot of money... ;)

And everything I am going to share with you is the REAL DEAL! If you ever would like to confirm who I am, just add me at www.facebook.com/7dayfitness and follow me or add me as a friend... I am one of the few celebrity trainers/authors who will personally welcome you and thank you for purchasing my book and give you some encouragement and tips as well. My life is truly a blessing and I want you to get a sneak peek on how I live my life to EXPECTEDLY encourage and motivate you to become better than your best.

After years of trying what works and what doesn't work, I have since reached and maintained an ideal weight with an amazing physique, in addition to boat loads of daily morning and after work evening energy. With a desirable physique that keeps the heads of the opposite sex turning daily. No worries; you will be showcasing your sexy sculpted body on the beaches of Jamaica as soon as you Take Action with the information you will read in just a second.

My doctor even told me that my health is so vibrant that diabetes, heart disease, cancer or high blood pressure will never be a part of my life, like it has affected so many in my family.

Pause one second... Before I go any further, please stop believing the Genetic bull shit! People use this term like they use ketchup on fries! It is not a genetic problem, the doctor and the media wants you to believe this, so you will feel you have no way out. LIES!! DAMN IT! ALL LIES! This will be explained in my book as well. It's going to shock you, so prepare yourself.

So let's get into it, so I can get you Slim and Trim without the long workouts and crazy late night rubber band inventions. And if you are a man or woman (no matter your age) after reading this book and use the strategies in the chapters below, you will be ready to mingle. And if you have a mate, after you take action today, your boo, guy or gal are going to drool over you like a married man at the strip club.

But before you believe a word that is printed in this book—or any book that sounds relevant to your life or resonates with you on any level—check them first! Research them! GOOGLE THEM!! Make sure they are not a fraud; there are so many frauds out there it blows my mind.

I can't name names, but there are many people who write FIT books, but they are not fit. They write how to be a millionaire books, but they are not millionaires!! You can find me at www.facebook.com/7dayfitness or do an easy Google search for Wesley Virgin and make sure I am congruent with the information you are about to be exposed to.

Wes Tip: Do this for any and every book you read in the future. I post and share my life experiences every day on my many social networks (Facebook, Twitter, and Instagram) to inspire you and let you know I am the real deal. My life is truly filled with kindness, love, care, gratitude, admiration and a unique obsession to serve the greater good.

My dream is for this book to not only inspire you, but cause an ultimate power to awaken within you; to fast-pace you into the body and life you desire and very much deserve.

1

Why Some People Get Results and Some Don't, and What to Do About It

Have you heard about the 3% versus the 97%? No? Well, let me explain. Have you ever noticed a person who always gets results, always gets the better part of the deal? There is a reason for this. There are two different types of people in the world... the 3%'s (the few who get in shape with ease and are constantly complimented about their appearance and physique) and... the 97%'s (the vast majority of the population who struggle and jump from program to program searching for the new and improved secret solution). I hate to tell you this, but the secret solution does not exist! But I will tell you what does and what doesn't work... 100 percent of the time.

Now, the simple strategy I am going to teach you below will help you be part of the 3%—The Fit and Sexy!

Let's play a game and I want you to be honest with me.

WHICH CATEGORY ARE YOU IN? THERE IS NO IN-BETWEEN, SO BE HONEST WITH YOURSELF!

The 97%:
- Make Excuses, Excuses and more Excuses
- Look for justifications and reasons why they can't make it happen!

- Are some of the world's biggest PROCRASTINATORS!
- Have No Drive! No Will! No Consistency!
- They pay for gym memberships, fitness DVDs and trainers but never use the services
- They always say, "I should do this..." rather than "I have to do this!!! I must do this!!!"
- Always use the two self-defeating words: "I can't!!!"
- Unfortunately they will never get it, and they will continue to stay up in the wee hours of the night only dreaming about an amazing body but never having it.

Now the 3% are different:

- They never make excuses! EVER!!
- Always see the water glass full, even when there is visibly not a single drop of water left.
- Have more reasons to succeed than REASONS to fail!
- Are always consistent NO MATTER WHAT!
- They don't hang with negative people
- Expect more from themselves every day
- Always see the positive side of a situation, challenge or issue
- They take MASSIVE ACTION every day, no paralysis analysis.
- If it looks good, sounds good and feels good, they pull the trigger!!
- They do the exact opposite of the 97%

Glad you're not in the 97%, right?! :) Or maybe you are is, no worries we are going to change that Today!!

Sounds interesting, right? Well, today I consider you to be

a 3% because not only did you decide to buy this book (Power Action Step), you have also taken an additional action step by reading the information and at the end applying the information that you will soon learn. Unfortunately, the 97%s are still procrastinating, searching the web and looking for the next quick fix. Story of their lives... But congrats, you are different!!! Keep reading.

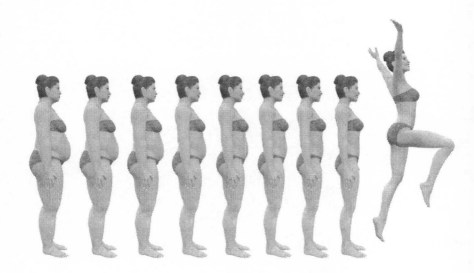

5 Tips You Need To Do NOW!!

- Take a second and think about why weight loss is so important to you. Why are you REALLY doing it? I want you to think hard for a second before answering... By the way, it is ok to be vain. Hell, I do it because I LOVE the attention and I LOVE looking at myself butt naked in the mirror!!! Now write down the reason that makes you smile, (keyword is SMILE) and put it in your wallet and your purse.
- After you write your reason, write down GET FIT

WITH PASSION at the end of it (this will make more sense after 30 days)

- Now, go to your computer and Google search someone that you deem to be physically attractive (I longed to have The Rock's physique, I even have his pic for inspiration on my bedroom wall, NO HOMO ;)) and post it on your mirror so you can see it every time you enter the bathroom and exit the shower.

- Finally, find an accountability partner, someone who will hold you accountable, maybe someone like Wesley Virgin or a super positive friend :). This is what I literally do full time, I don't only design 7-minute workouts, but I am there to get you going and keep you motivated during the first 30 days of starting this process. I am going to be in your ear, in your email, on your Facebook page every day until your body is hot enough to lay close to butt naked on the beautiful beaches of Miami! I am relentless!!! I'll talk more about this later.

- Do this now before proceeding on. Go to my Facebook page at www.facebook.com/7DayFitness or go to www.7DayFitness.com and let me know you have completed these 5 simple steps. This is a behaviour and habit of the 3%.   :)

Ok, I need you to read my next statement very closely and carefully. You are not going to believe my next statement. As a matter of fact I might get into trouble but let me tell you the real deal about fitness infomercials and the industry itself.

Do you remember those Sunday nights after all the partying, drinking and hanging with friends you find yourself sitting on the couch thinking about the next work day? And then it happens, you see the fitness infomercials of the so called experts telling you to purchase their fitness program. But not just that!!! They persuade you with testimonies and before and after pictures (that are fake) and convincing stories that will make anyone make an emotional buying decision.

Check this out. After doing my research I found out that they actually hire a group of people who would like to lose weight and go through their fitness program (their results will be used for the infomercial of course).

They take pictures, record videos and gather all the material to make a... DRUM ROLL PLEASE!!

A LATE NIGHT FITNESS INFOMERCIAL!

A late night sales video designed to cajole you into purchasing yet another DVD program that you will only use for a week!! IF THAT!

Now don't get me wrong, the programs are great for TEENAGERS and people who will actually use them!! But for the hard working, no time having, parents like myself, it is definitely not for us. Many of the DVD in the box programs use a lot of plyometrics which means lots of joint and back pain for you in the near future. And I do not know about you, but I am not a fan of the joint and back pain.

I remember the first day I did INSANITY (a workout routine), just to impress this super cute chick I met at my apartment. Let's just say after Day 1 of doing the Insanity routine, I decided she wasn't all that cute and definitely wasn't worth the pain of continuing with Mr. Shaun T.

So what do I do, Wes?

Well, the next time you see those types of infomercials that are designed for you to buy, but not designed for you to GET THE BODY OF YOUR DREAMS, turn it off and search for a fitness program that will provide motivation and constant encouragement!! And everyday interaction!! I have learned in the past 10 years that most Superstars (I hate the word clients) just want to know that someone genuinely cares.

You know... Most people lose motivation because they run out of gas, not because they don't want it bad enough. For example, if you go to the gas station and fill up your tank to the F and travel back and forth from work, which is a combined two hour commute, and do not refuel. It doesn't matter how bad you want that car to move, if you have no gas (aka motivation), you are not going anywhere. You are going to be stuck on the side of the road with your thumb out! This is the exact same thing that happens when we start workout programs. We get the DVD, buy the cute or hot workout clothes, get hyped up, and tell our friends that we are going to lose 10, 20 or even 30 pounds for our next vacation... Then for some reason we lose the fire, we lose the motivation, we lose the will to keep pushing ourselves.

YOU NEED THE GAS!! You need someone in your ear, but most of all you need to have a compelling Why! I really deep dive into this in the following chapters, but without the Why, you will fail. Did you notice those 2 munchkins (my kiddos) you saw in the beginning of this book, THAT IS MY WHY!! I love them and I am not going to be a good example for them. I am GOING TO BE A GREAT EXAMPLE FOR THEM!!

Superstar (talking to you), there isn't any struggle when it comes to losing weight. There isn't any struggle trying to create a physique that your creator would like you to have.

After watching the superstars at my boot camp and the tens of thousands of people I train online every day, there is a very distinct difference in the ones that fail and the ones that soar. It is their reasons, their "Why."

I remember when I used get traffic tickets for stupid careless reasons. No license, no insurance, no tags, speeding, super dark tint. LOL!! Literally, I was stopped and pulled over by the police at least once a night (chasing this hot girl I wanted to bang) and he would give me a ticket every night, and of course I couldn't pay it. And I told the judge exactly what we all tell the judge when he starts slapping on court cost and ridiculous fines... I do not have the money, Sir! Did he care? Hell no.

No Money = Jail Time!!

It's so funny. We get upset at other people when we know it is our fault. I used to get mad at the officer, the judge, lawyer, even the chick I was driving across town to pick up. But it was me the entire time, failing to take responsibility of my actions and failing to stand up and take ownership of all my mishaps and wrongdoings.

Are you getting my point here? It is time for you to take OWNERSHIP OF YOUR BODY AND YOUR LIFE!!

I still repeat and have many of my VIP Superstars repeat this as well. Try it.

ALL I NEED IS WITHIN ME NOW!!
ALL I NEED IS WITHIN ME NOW!!
ALL I NEED IS WITHIN ME NOW!!

ALL I NEED IS WITHIN ME NOW!!
ALL I NEED IS WITHIN ME NOW!!
ALL I NEED IS WITHIN ME NOW!!
ALL I NEED IS WITHIN ME NOW!!

I know you are enthralled in this book right now, but I would like you to get up right now. GET UP!! RIGHT NOW! STAND UP, SUPERSTAR!! Go to the mirror and tell yourself the phrases below:

1. I am taking action today!
2. I don't make excuses.
3. I am becoming a better me.
4. I am creating a delicious tastefully sculpted body NOW!
5. I will not blame anyone for anything that happens in my life.
6. I am a Superstar.
7. I am Powerful!!!
8. I am Gorgeous!
9. I am Beautiful!
10. I am Significant!
11. I am giving my GOD'S best EVERY single Day of my Life!

Notice, I use language that is spoken in the NOW. They are powerful "I AM" statements. Stop staying I want to, I should, I am going to. Eliminate those 3 from your vocabulary today!!

Say those 11 statements with power and conviction. Do this every day while you in the bathroom for 30 days (just 30 days). After 30 days you will start to think differently. You will start to associate with different people. You will see life as a blessing instead of an entitlement. People will start to gravitate to you and they will agree and validate with your thoughts. And one day you will not only create the most amazing body of your life. You will discover how every aspect in your life will soar!! Financial abundance!!! Happy Wife! Happy Husband! Happy Children!! Great and Happy Relationships! Closer spiritual connection with your creator!

How do I know this?

Because I am living and experiencing the pure sweet juice of life every single day. Say yes!!!! Remember to take immediate action, you will never be the same. Remember you can always chat with me at www.7DayFitness.com. I would love to meet you.

2

When You Read This Chapter You Will Cancel Your Gym Membership

I am going to make this chapter quick and to the point. We believe the longer we bust our butts in the gym, the sooner we will see results, and this may be true, but is this something you really want do? Hmm, No!!! Tell me what man or woman is going to keep up with a 55-minute routine for the rest of their lives? Maybe a body builder or a superstar athlete! But they have an incentive!! They are getting paid to bust their butts, joints and back, they are getting paid millions for this, LOL.

How much are you getting paid for this? Not a damn dime!!!

So I would like you to take a second and think about the trainer and gym world. What is their #1 responsibility? What is the one thing that they MUST do each and every day?

Guessed?

Yep, you are right… Make Money!!

Think about how it relates to your current job or profession. You are not going to work every morning fighting traffic because you love your boss, co-workers and the Friday morning free donuts. No!!! You are there to get your check at the end of the week, every other week, or at the end of the month. So trainers and gyms are the same, they focus their attention on making a dollar.

When was the last time your trainer or your gym facility texted you or called you to give you some much needed encouragement or motivation when you wanted to quit? Hmmmm?? Never, Wes!!

Remember trainers are just like you. After high school or college, we need a job to make money. Sooooo we are looking and searching for a profession to take care of our family. So then most trainers take a weekend or month-long class to get certified and voila! They are a certified personal trainer.

The problem is this. The trainer may know about workouts, routines, exercises and verbally spit out convoluted industry jargon like ligaments and abdominal rectus, but they have no idea how to strategically motivate a person who has tried everything, who is disappointed, mildly depressed and who is on the brink of giving up.

Gym's and trainer's sole responsibility is to keep billing you monthly, not designing new programs to ensure your success, not taking you by the hand and showing love and compassion through the process.

When I created the www.7DayFitness.com system, I knew

I was missing something because people were losing their motivation and drive. So just recently, I spent a ton of money creating a Motivational Buddy System where a new superstar can select someone just like themselves, to keep them motivated during their journey.

Say you are a mom with children and more than one job, well then you find another mom with children and more than one job. Say if you are over the age of 40 and have all types of joint pains and back pains. Well, you can find someone just like you who has joint and back pain issues but still transformed their body and their lives. How cool is that?

I will urge you to cancel your current gym membership if you are not using it. Seriously they are billing you as you are reading this book. I also urge you to fire your trainer, if for (1) they are not fit and (2) they do not understand your unique issues or workout issues.

Test you can take right now to see if your gym or trainer isn't working: (If you have a gym membership or a trainer I would like you do something for me right now.)

1. Go to the bathroom and lock the door (this is private stuff).
2. Take off all of your clothes. Everything!
3. Look at every inch of your body for 5 minutes straight. Are you smiling or frowning?
4. If you are smiling than you are there my friend and I wish you all the best!!
5. But if you are frowning and feel a bit discouraged. LOOK YOURSELF IN THE MIRROR RIGHT NOW!!
6. Tell yourself these words: I AM A WINNER!! I AM A SUPERSTAR! I AM GORGEOUS!! I (INSERT NAME)

YOU HAVE AN AMAZING BODY!! GET FIT WITH PASSION

7. Then proceed to pick up the phone, call your bank and cancel your gym membership and tell your trainer he or she is FIRED!! Great feeling!!!

8. Sounds weird, I know. BUT IT WORKS!! Everyone who works and trains with me goes through this exact same process. You can also see many videos of 7DayFit Superstars cancelling their gym memberships at www.7dayfitness.com/blog

Unfortunately society has conditioned us that a trainer and a gym is the only route to an amazing body. Newsflash!! It's the twenty-first century! And there are several new innovative ways to fast pace results that will allow you to jump into the body that receives endless amounts of compliments from the opposite sex. Maybe these gyms and trainers will try to sue me after reading this book, but so what! You deserve to know the truth and you deserve to have a trainer who cares about you.

Question: Why does Insanity and P90x cost hundreds of dollars when all they give you is a bunch of DVD's and some workout logs? Then on the other hand my DVD program is only 40 bucks with fewer DVD's inclusive of a mindset DVD (which is worth over 500 bucks because it teaches you how to condition your mind to ensure the journey is super easy)?

Actually I wanted to be the first trainer in the world to actually produce, video, edit and DVD author his own program. I did it all. I even found a few hot chicks that you will see on my DVD here at www.7dayfitnessprogram.com who assisted me to make this program a success. Thanks Tahjy, Cortney and Cece!!! I love you all!!

How I got the attention of Oprah and Tyler Perry

But let me tell you a story that almost pissed off Tyler Perry and Oprah Winfrey. Now to be clear, I think Tyler Perry and Oprah Winfrey are some of the most genuine, inspiring and giving people on the earth!! But Tyler almost pissed me off and you will see why in a second.

Now I, Wesley Virgin, believe in taking massive action. I learned this technique from my buddy Tony Robbins. Sooooo I did... Now Tyler and Oprah are super famous they probably have many layers in front of them before you could ever speak to them.

I have sent Oprah Facebook comments and messages; so many that now I am banned from posting comments on her page, LOL. I even made a crazy hilarious video on YouTube that you can see here www.7dayfitness.com/oprahloveswes. Lots of love from other people but no Oprah.

So I was thinking to myself, how can I get Tyler Perry's and Oprah's attention to at least open up my 7-Minute DVD package and check out my secret sauce? So I got it! Now you might think this technique is a bit unethical but I had to be an Outlier and think outside the box!! So I mailed the entire 7DayFitness DVD set to Tyler Perry's Studios but I wrote on the envelope in care of the OWN Network. LOL!

Now look at the email I received from Madea's office...

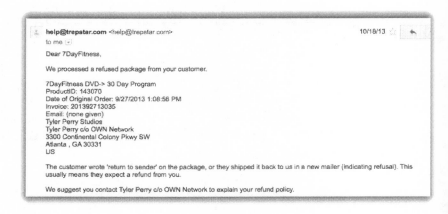

But if you prefer to use P90x and Insanity which are back breaking workouts in my opinion, then go ahead, my fitness system is designed in 7-minute increments to lose, lean and to be seen!!

Yep, they rejected my package! For a fraction of a second, I could have gotten pissed off, but to my surprise, I was excited. Tyler Perry actually looked at my package! He didn't open it, but at least he saw the www.7DayFitness.com brand.

So the point is that I had to persevere! I had to reframe the negative response I received from Tyler Perry's office to a positive response.

When you begin your get-sexy journey, the rain and the storm will come, but what makes a 3% a true rock star is he or she runs through the storm. And he or she doesn't carry an umbrella and he or she is not thinking about the lightning and the dangers of the water. He perseveres and becomes impervious to all adverse conditions.

It is your time, my friend. Run through the storm because the California sunny beach weather is waiting for you on the other side.

3

The Two Biggest Workout Mistakes
You Have Probably Already Committed

1. Plyometrics

So, most of us over the age of 30 are experiencing all types of knee, back and joint pain. This is called Life!!! :)

So the challenge was for me to create a system that was effective but didn't kill my joints or my back. There are certain routines you should absolutely avoid! I will list one below…

Just Say No To Plyometrics. Stay away from long distance running, treadmills, running and banging your bones on concrete and be cautious of P90x and Insanity (your decision). These routines are pure death if you have bad knees, joints or back problems. Now do not get me wrong. I take my hat off to Tony and Shaun T but obviously Insanity and P90x is not one-size-fits-all program. And remember they are just the puppets, there is a huge production company with billions of dollars who are marketing and promoting to drive the sales.

But let me educate ya…

What is Plyometrics, Wes?

It is basically a lot of jumping, which damages your knees dramatically!

Now don't get me wrong, these programs do work, but they use a lot of plyometric type routines. Plyometric routines create a lot of pressure on your joints, knees and back, and they are not designed for people like you and me. So yes! You will lose weight, slowly of course, but all at the expense of your bones and joints.

Now maybe back in our 20's, when we were invincible; jumping over fences and playing sports till the sun went down, but now in my 30's, my knees and back are talking to me. They're saying, "Hello Wesley, what are you doing!!! Stop jumping around like a crazy person!!"

There are numerous medical studies that confirm the cartilage that is located between your joints will eventually deteriorate as you get older, which is normal. But many types of intense, back-breaking programs that you see on TV and YouTube are for teenagers. They are not designed for the average guy or gal over the age of 30 that has had multiple knee injuries, back injuries and surgeries in those areas.

This is the reason why most people roll out of bed in the morning, because their knees and back are killing them after using joint intense fitness programs!

Let me tell you how important your back is.

The back is the foundation of the body, involved in almost every activity from running, walking, taking out the trash, washing the car, dancing and even carrying your beautiful children.

Stop taking pills for your aches and pains. Our body is designed to heal itself. But you have to do the correct type of exercises.

I am going to give you one routine that I do at least 5 times a week to strengthen my lower back. You can try it out for free here www.7dayfitness.com/home-workout-to-regenerate-lower-back-pains/.

Would you believe me if I told you that working out less is more beneficial than spending hours in the gym? Let me explain. The industry standard for the last 30 years has been working out for 45 minutes to an hour. Just think about it, if that was true then why is the US alone the most obese country in the world? I mean, I know several people who work-out for hours, but they are still overweight, fat, and still have that stubborn poochie pooch! LOL! So obviously length of time is not the key to develop long-term muscle and eliminate stubborn fat.

Listen closely. Use this statement on your next workout and the next time you work-out.

It is not how much you do! It is how often you get it done. I have been drilling this in people's heads for years. Why do you think I call my company 7DayFitness? Because it is a habitual lifestyle. Just like driving to work, taking a shower, having a late night drink or having nightly great sex. You want your workouts and routine to be rooted so deep in your subconscious mind that you don't have to think about it. I will talk more about the conditioning of your subconscious mind in my next book.

2. Running

So I am going to go out on a limb and say that you do not like running. Personally, I hate it!! I did it in the military and I hated every minute of it. I am not a runner and I do not enjoy it...

And let me make something clear, running is not going to burn the amount of fat in a short period of time.

Let me educate you real quickly on how the body works and how we actually lose weight.

First of all, this is very rudimentary if you think about it. If you want to lose fat or weight, something needs to be removed from your body, correct? The only way to see the scale take a nose dive is either by sweating it out through your pores or you are going to do it the savvy way and have several bowel movements (aka Boo Boo) to get the waste and toxins out of your body.

Our bodies are so toxic and so adulterated with germs, toxins, chemicals, metals and the list goes on. Running miles and getting on the treadmill is not going to extract enough sweat or toxins from your body for the scale to take a nose dive. In fact, why would you want all of that fecal matter and unwanted toxins coming out of your pores anyway? Disgusting!!

Now, if running is your thing, do it! But if you're trying to lose 10% of your body fat in the next 30 to 60 days, there is an alternate routine I suggest you do.

So like I explained above, running is what we have been conditioned to believe to lose fat or lose weight. Everyone still associates cardio to running. I hear it all the time from very unfit people at the gym. Honestly, running sucks and it is not the most intelligent way to lose weight. The only time you will ever see Wesley Virgin running is when I am playing hide-go-seek with my amazing kids or running behind some super-hot chick on Venice Beach!!! ;)

So your question is this. What type of cardio workouts can I do, Wes, to lose weight fast?

Easy!! Go get yourself a jump rope!! Yes a super inexpensive jump rope! I love the jump rope! I adore the jump rope! I swear the jump rope is responsible for shredding my abs and leaning me out to perfection. I am not trying brag or boast but it's the truth. The jump rope rapidly speeds up your heart rate and it also flushes out the lymphatic system.

Now the key to using the jump rope is not to bang your feet against the ground. When I first started I used to jump as if I was jumping over hurdles, but I quickly learned all you needed was a very small hop. The champ Floyd Mayweather taught me this. This guy is such an inspiration and a beast when it comes to the rope and putting a whipping on his opponents!!

I have more detailed routines on my website at www.7dayfitness.com but I am going to give you a simple routine right now that you can follow for the next 7 days.

❖ Monday- Thursday:
  Upon Rising Drink a Full Glass of Evamor or Spring Water
  Jump rope for 7 minutes (first thing in the morning before work)

By doing this in the morning, it will elevate your mood and it should cause you to go to the bathroom as well (**Note:** you want to boo boo at least three times a day).

That is it, no more, no less.

So that is it. No more running and no more plyometrics type routines, stop banging your joints against the concrete! The jump rope is your friend and you will lose more fat plus you will awaken hidden energy and rapidly increase your daily endurance.

Personally, I have the same amount of energy at 8am, noon, evening and even late night. You will notice on my Instagram and Facebook pages, I post videos and workouts in the wee hours of the night. I swear to you, my body has never felt so energized after being introduced to the jump rope. Now let's get to the good stuff, let me show you my little secret which, they would prefer me not to say.

Wes who are *they*? Hmmmm. Well let me give you a hint. It is a 3-letter word and you can possibly be sent to prison if you tell the truth about their practices. My lips are sealed! LOL…

Turn to the next chapter…

4

2 Secret Foods That Make Fat Melt

Ok this chapter is going to excite you! It is going to finally answer the question that millions have asked for decades.

Is it possible to lose lots of weight (at least 30 lbs.) without stepping foot in the gym? Hell Yea!!! Are you smiling? You should be because the 2 superfoods that I am going to share with you are going to change your life and your thinking as it relates to weight loss.

These two items are far better than any pill, potion or lotion on earth!!! You will lose weight, have an abundance of energy and have the youthful vitality you had when you were a child.

But I am going to be honest with you. Most foods in the western civilization are pure trash. Chemicals, GMOs, Pesticides, Herbicides, Larvaside and Fungicide are lurking in almost every meal you eat these days. But I have great news. These powerful superfoods of the future are going to destroy all the toxins, metals and acids that are in your body in the next 30 days. Yes it only takes 30 days! You are going to drop weight super quickly, if you follow the easy to-do steps below, even if you have a burger, a slice of homemade pie or even a slice of your favorite pizza. These super powders will reverse your current situation in 30 short days along with massive amounts of weight loss.

Wheatgrass

The first hidden food I would like to introduce you to is wheatgrass. No, I am not talking about the grass on your front lawn, wheatgrass is probably the most powerful source of chlorophyll on the planet.

Ok Wes, are you speaking in Chinese? Break it down in layman's terms. Well 1 scoop of wheatgrass is equivalent to 5 servings of uncooked vegetables.

I take wheatgrass daily in the form of a powder twice a day, mixed with spring water or coconut water. One time in the morning, and one time in the evening. This is basically pure chlorophyll which is the sun's energy!!!

Did I mention that this is 5 servings of veggies per scoop! Most of us feel we are eating our veggies but did you know even if you lightly steam your vegetables you are killing the live enzymes in the food. Eating a diet that contains at least 50% of raw foods is the key to ensure you extract all of the toxins from your body.

This scoop of excellence will neutralize toxins in your body in the first week, aka fat loss every 7 days. And the weight will begin to fall off even without doing any cardio. :) But you should still do some form of working out to Tone, Lean and Sculpt. But the fat loss is going to be a cinch!!

Here is a List of Juicy and Exciting Benefits:

➢ **Increases red blood-cell** count and lowers blood pressure. It cleanses the blood, organs and gastrointestinal tract of debris.

Wheatgrass also stimulates metabolism and the body's enzyme systems by enriching the blood. It also aids in reducing blood pressure by dilating the blood pathways throughout the body.

➢ **Stimulates the thyroid gland, correcting obesity, indigestion and a host of other complaints.**

➢ **Restores alkalinity to the blood.** The juice's abundance of alkaline minerals helps reduce over-acidity in the blood. It can be used to relieve many internal pains, and has been used successfully to treat peptic ulcers, ulcerative colitis, constipation, diarrhea, and other complaints of the gastrointestinal tract.

➢ **Is a powerful detoxifier, and liver and blood protector.**

➢ The enzymes and amino acids found in wheatgrass can protect us from carcinogens like no other food or medicine. It strengthens our cells, detoxifies the liver and bloodstream, and chemically neutralizes environmental pollutants.

➢ **When used as a rectal implant, reverses damage from inside the lower bowel.** An implant is a small amount of juice held in the lower bowel for about 20 minutes. In the case of illness, wheatgrass implants stimulate a rapid cleansing of the lower bowel and draw out accumulations of debris.

➢ Externally applied to the skin can **help eliminate itching** almost immediately.

➢ **Will soothe sunburned skin and act as a disinfectant.** Rubbed into the scalp before a shampoo, it will help mend damaged hair and alleviate itchy, scaly, scalp conditions.

➢ **Works as a sleep aide.** Merely place a tray of living wheatgrass near the head of your bed. It will enhance the oxygen in the air and generate healthful negative ions to help you sleep more soundly.

➢ **Enhances your bath.** Add some to your bath water and settle in for a nice, long soak.

➢ **Sweetens the breath** and firms up and tightens gums. Just gargle with the juice.

➢ **Neutralizes toxic substances** like cadmium, nicotine, strontium, mercury, and polyvinyl chloride.

➢ **Offers the benefits of a liquid oxygen transfusion since the juice contains liquid oxygen.** Oxygen is vital to many body processes: it stimulates digestion (the oxidation of food), promotes clearer thinking (the brain utilizes 25% of the body's oxygen supply), and protects the blood against anaerobic bacteria.

➢ **Turns gray hair to its natural colour** again and greatly increases energy levels when consumed daily.

➢ **Is a beauty treatment that slows down the aging process** when the juice is consumed. Wheatgrass will cleanse your blood and help rejuvenate aging cells, slowing the aging process way down, making you feel more alive right away. It will help tighten loose and sagging skin.

➢ **Restores fertility and promotes youthfulness.**

30-Day INTAKE INSTRUCTIONS:

❖ Take 1 Scoop of Wheatgrass in the morning and 1 scoop in the evening. I mix mine with orange juice (organic, not bottled), spring water, coconut water or I will use my blender to juice a few fruits to dilute the taste ;)

If you have any concerns or questions, you can always chat with me at www.facebook.com/7DayFitness.

Cacao Powder

Do you like chocolate? Sure you do, but did you now that not only is it a powerful aphrodisiac, it is said to be the most pure form of vitamin C! Cacao is a raw form of chocolate but has all the nutrients and cofactors we miss on a daily diet. Cacao is literally one of the strongest antioxidants on earth. Basically this will keep you from getting sick and reducing your allergies by 90% if you continually consume cacao on a daily basis. Personally I use almond milk and stir one tablespoon twice a day (morning and evening) and drink this coco delish beverage daily.

Wesley, will this give me the morning energy like my hot morning coffee? Yes, this will replace coffee and give you twice the amount of energy than the acidic caffeine you are drinking.

What Wesley, no more coffee?

Kick coffee to the curb, because it is highly acidic and it can possibly do some long-term damage to your internal body functions.

Here are the Benefits:

➢ **Antioxidants:** Cacao has more antioxidant flavonoids than any food tested so far, including blueberries, red wine, and black and green teas. In fact, it has up to four times the quantity of antioxidants found in green tea. Health benefits of these antioxidants include:

- **Promote Heart health** - Help dilate bloods vessels, reduce blood clotting, improve circulation, help regulate heartbeat and blood pressure, lower LDL cholesterol, and reduce the risk of stroke and heart attacks.

- **Protect from environmental toxins** - Help repair and resist damage caused by free radicals, and reduces the risk of certain cancers.

➢ **The Feel Good Bean:** By increasing the levels of specific neurotransmitters in our brains, cacao promotes positive outlook, facilitates rejuvenation and simply helps us feel good.

- **Serotonin** - Cacao raises the level of serotonin in the brain; thus acts as an anti-depressant, helps reduce PMS symptoms, and promotes a sense of well-being.

- **Endorphins** - Cacao stimulates the secretion of endorphins, producing a pleasurable sensation similar to the "runner's high" a jogger feels after running several miles.

- **Phenylethylamine** - Found in chocolate, phenylethylamine is also created within the brain and released when we are in love. Acts as mild mood elevator and anti-depressant, and helps increase focus and alertness.

- **Anandamide** - Anandamide is known as the "bliss chemical" because it is released by the brain when we are feeling great. Cacao contains both N-acylethanolamines, believed to temporarily increase the levels of anandamide in the brain, and enzyme inhibitors that slow its breakdown. Promotes relaxation, and helps us feel good longer.

➢ **Essential Minerals:** Cacao beans are rich in a number of essential minerals, including magnesium, sulfur, calcium, iron, zinc, copper, potassium and manganese.

- **Magnesium** - Cacao seems to be the #1 source of magnesium of any food. Magnesium balances brain chemistry, builds strong bones, and helps regulate heartbeat and blood pressure. Magnesium deficiency, present in 80% of Americans, is linked with PMT, hypertension, heart disease, diabetes and joint problems.

- **Sulfur** - Cacao is high in the beauty mineral sulfur. Sulfur builds strong nails and hair, promotes beautiful skin, detoxifies the liver, and supports healthy pancreas functioning.

➢ **Essential fats:** There is a misperception that chocolate is fattening. In truth, the fats in cocoa butter are healthy fats. Cacao contains oleic acid, a heart-healthy monounsaturated fat, also found in olive oil that may raise good cholesterol. Also, substances found in cacao are known to help reduce appetite.

➢ **Appetite suppressant:** Yes, that's right! Raw chocolate actually has appetite-suppressant properties and often added to weight loss products to help control hunger! Simply enjoy a couple of Raw CHOC's or add half a teaspoon of raw chocolate powder to a teacup of tepid water 10 minutes before a meal for a delicious, natural way to reduce your appetite.

➢ **Aphrodisiac:** Chocolate has long been the food for lovers and is a symbol of sensuality and sexuality. The ancient Aztecs gave chocolate as wedding presents and other South American civilizations believed that chocolate was the food of the heart.

Raw chocolate from South America has to be the best chocolate aphrodisiac about!

➢ **Sense of wellbeing:** Long considered a 'happy food', chocolate is a popular treat when we need 'cheering up.' Recent research has discovered that cacao contains chemicals (such as Phenylethylamine* and Serotonine) which are scientifically proven to be present in the brains of people when they are happy, more relaxed, playful and creative.

30-Day INTAKE INSTRUCTIONS:

❖ Mix with almond milk or water or you can juice with fruits or veggies, 1 tablespoon in 8 oz of the beverage I listed above, 1 time in the morning and 1 time in the evening. As soon as you get up you should take this after consuming a glass of Evamor water and right before you go to sleep, have another drink

WESLEY's ALL IN ONE SOLUTION

Now if you are like me, have children, work, church, sports, school, social life and are just basically super busy, you can combine the two super foods together in a smoothie or just use a glass of spring water.

I typically use water, coconut water or freshly squeezed orange juice to give the drink some taste.

30-Day INTAKE INSTRUCTIONS:

- ❖ Drink a full glass of evamor or spring water first.
- ❖ Mix 1 tablespoon of each powder together in the morning with fresh orange juice, coconut water or just take out your blender and juice with veggies (pineapple, strawberries, blueberries, grapes, kale, spinach or spring mix are my fav).
- ❖ Do this consistently for 30 days and I promise you... Promise you!! Guarantee you!! You will lose at least 10% of your body fat in the first 30 to 60 days!!

So now you have it. The secret is out of the bag! Now it is time for you to take action!

5

Powerful Celebrity Secret
Which Gives You a Great Sex Life

So let's be honest here!! We have all experienced times when our performance in the bedroom was an embarrassment and a disgrace. Trust me! I have been there as well. Most men visit the drug stores or even the guy around the corner in the alley that gives us the little blue pill. But after 5 years of research, and following some of my favorite Foodism Guru's, I found a better and pure natural way.

This superfood that I am about to reveal will help your body reach an alkaline state quickly, which basically means it will neutralize toxins out of the body so the scale can take a consistent nose dive while keeping the body part between your legs hot and ready for action. (Sorry, but I told you I was not going to filter my words.) It increases sexual energy like nobody's business. I don't want to be obscene or graphic here but let's just say this, I'm almost 40 and after taking this powdery superfood my sex drive is 10,000 times better without any over-the-counter stimulation. LOL

It is true that we all want to cut the fat, of course. But why not have long lasting, passionate hot sex as well!? Of course!! Sex is probably the most amazing emotion that our creator has allowed us to experience. This powdery goodness will increase your libido and endurance in men and women.

The 4-letter word is Maca!! After reading this chapter, visit www.7dayfitness.com/maca to read more about it and get a bag!

Women get ready to Jump for Joy!!!!

Maca exponentially boosts the mood in women after a long stressful day dealing with the crazy girl that is trying to get you fired. Maca also relieves menstrual issues and menopause. Ladies, are you smiling yet!! Say goodbye to the monthly pain while on your period and the morning and afternoon cramps that we men will never understand. It alleviates cramps, body pain, hot flashes, anxiety, mood swings, and depression. But I must warn you, if you are pregnant or lactating you should consult with a doctor first. Maca clears your skin of acne and blemishes (in all climates) no matter if you are down south in Houston, TX or far north in Ontario, Canada

This is one of the little secrets that celebrities use consistently to keep their physique TV-hot and youthful after 40 and even 50 years of age. Hell, look at Janet Jackson and Halle Berry!! If they happen to divorce again, I promise you, I am next inline. LOL

Personally I am addicted to the Maca powder! After taking the Maca powder, any man would love to feel the vitality and the response from his woman and he will be addicted as well! Not just because of the great sex and having the ability to show his woman who's the boss in the bedroom. No No No!!! But to have the energy and vitality to enjoy your cute munchkins as you play for hours at the park. Get your bag of maca today, in the link below I give you the exact brand I purchase...

Read more about the benefits of Maca powder here www.7dayfitness.com/maca.

6

The 1# Secret Elixir Fixer

So in this chapter I am going to give you something that has, in my opinion, been hidden from the masses for years. Especially in the States. (Yes! Even Decades!) In this new age there are so many discoveries that are being exposed that great people like you need to be aware of.

But before I start to verbally vomit about this super serum, let me tell you exactly what it did for me. As you may know I love to workout but after the age of 34 my body started to ache more than usual and the muscle soreness became unbearable at times. Actually I thought it was my pillows and bed at one time, so I went out and bought a $2,000 dollar mattress, and then I bought a $100 pillow.

Waste of money!!

To say the least, none of this worked, my friend. Now in all honestly when I started to take this all-natural super serum, I had no idea it would cure my body aches but it also decreased the after workout soreness that so many of us dread. This stuff over exceeded my expectations 100 times over. Even though I was aging it felt like my body was reversing the aging process.

Ok so let me tell you what it is because like I said before, I am not going to bore you with futile abject information. I am going to give you the strategy and the technique immediately.

Marine Phytoplankton!!

Phyto what? ;)

Marine Phytoplankton is a unique, live ultra-nutrient rich product similar to foods like spirulina in that they both have been on our planet for billions of years. It's likely to be the next biggest thing when it comes to superfoods, so if you haven't heard about it until now, expect to be hearing a lot more in the near future.

Like all microalgae grown in the ocean, this particular strain was specifically chosen for its potent health benefits. It is only one of four species of Marine Phytoplankton found to be beneficial for human consumption.

This supercharged micro-algae is a living food and enzyme active. It contains every known mineral and all of the amino acids our body needs to achieve optimal health. It is also the original source of Omega-3s – even more powerful than the popular, well-known sources like fish or flax oil.

Just some of its many benefits include:

- ✓ Boosting the immune system
- ✓ Enhanced brain function
- ✓ Anti-inflammatory support
- ✓ Improved cellular repair
- ✓ Antibacterial, antiviral and antifungal effects
- ✓ Improved cardiovascular system
- ✓ Allergy relief

This powerful food is even able to provide an instant energy boost from its essential fatty acids. Unlike most foods out there, which takes time to be converted in our body before the energy can be utilized, the nutrition from Marine Phytoplankton is literally delivered directly into the blood stream in only a few seconds.

In addition to its powerful nutrients, minerals and amino acids, it contains hundreds of different carotenoids as well as hundreds of potent phytochemicals. These elements work together to protect your body's issues as well as to remove toxins and detoxify the blood. They can even reverse abnormal cell division that may lead to cancer.

Marine Phytoplankton can help fight a long list of health conditions, including:

- o Cancers
- o Rheumatoid arthritis
- o Type-2 diabetes
- o Heart disease
- o Skin disorders
- o Alzheimer's and other age-related diseases
- o Depression
- o Liver disease
- o Chronic Fatigue Syndrome
- o Infertility and other reproductive system disorders
- o Chronic pain, including joint pain

All this greatness in just 4 small drops a day, as it comes in a liquid form. Let me give you the facts about Marine Phytoplankton.

MARINE PHYTOPLANKTON NUTRITIONAL FACTS:

- ✓ Contains higher amounts of omega-3 fatty acids than fish.
- ✓ Over 200 types of chlorophyll rich plankton nutrients
- ✓ Over 200 sea vegetables

✓ 400 times the energy of any known plant
✓ Contains nearly every vitamin, mineral, amino acid, co-enzyme, enzyme, and antioxidant needed for survival.
✓ Marine phytoplankton is pH alkaline that can help balance a person's pH level.

Now in my opinion everyone should be purchasing this stuff and adding it to your daily intake. Oh yea! If you have a craving that you would like to get rid of, take the Marine Phytoplankton. There are so many nutrients in this serum that your body will not auto crave at night. The reason why most of us crave food is because we basically have malnutrition; I am not talking about the person that vomits after every meal. When you eat at fast foods places and restaurants, most of the nutritional value is nonexistent.

It just tastes good!! Marine Phytoplankton along with all the others superfoods I shared with you, will keep your body alkalized and healthy even when you take a few cheat days. You can read more about acidic vs. alkaline here at www.7dayfitness.com/acidic-vs-alkaline/.

Let me show you what else it does:

Supports Cardiovascular Health: The high level of antioxidants, amino acids, and high levels of omega-3 fatty acids are known to support a healthier cardiovascular system.

Promotes Healthy Skin: There are large amounts of bioflavonoids that can remove toxins from skin cells. Marine phytoplankton also contains riboflavin that reduces free radical attacks in skin cells.

Helps to Reduce High Cholesterol: High cholesterol is a problem millions of Americans deal with. Niacin, gamma linoleic acid and omega-3 fatty acids help to reduce high cholesterol.

Boosts the Immune System: Alanine, beta-carotene, bioflavonoids, and vitamin E are all immune system enhancers found in this superfood.

Increase Energy: Marine phytoplankton detoxifies the body, and eliminates toxins from the cells. This will improve your energy and mood levels.

Stabilizes Blood Sugar Levels: Marine phytoplankton is really good for stabilizing blood sugar levels. Chromium helps to prevent and moderate against diabetes. Glutamic acids help to reduce alcohol and sugar cravings. Phenylalanine is a known sugar craving reducer.

Increases Vision: Beta-carotene is a cornea protector, and improves vision function.

Helps with Joint Health: It will help a lot with joint mobility, and reducing pain and stiffness. Manganese helps to assist in joint mobility. Omega-6 fatty acids can relieve symptoms of arthritis. Pathohenic acid can reduce morning pain caused by arthritis.

Liver Support: Arginine is found in this superfood and is known to help detoxify the liver. It will go right through the liver, and into the blood stream.

Improves Brain Function: The high amount of omega-3 fatty acids improve brain function. The nucleic acids can enhance the memory. Phenylalanine improves mental clarity. Proline increases learning ability. Magnesium helps reduce mood swings.

Now most of us are not going to stop eating burgers, fries, pizza, ice cream, chips and all the other tasty foods in the world. Right? I have great news for you, you do not have to quit 100%, you can have a delightful snack, in moderation of-course, along with a shot of Marine Phytoplankton and the other superfoods I gave you in the previous chapters, and you will be good to go!!

Have you ever wondered why the flu season is so seasonal? The only reason why we catch the flu, get sick or have uncontrollable allergies is because of a deficient immune system. You don't need a freaking shot at your local drug store. I haven't been sick or experienced a headache in years.

Remember all the foods and liquids that we ingest have to be digested in our body and most of the foods our culture consumes metabolizes into an acidic ash. Unfortunately most foods that we eat are extremely acidic so after years of ingesting acidic food like dairy, meat, junk food and etc., one day in your 30s or 40s your doctor will possibly diagnose you with high blood pressure, diabetes or even worse, heart disease. This all can be prevented if you follow my simple daily steps below:

1. Purchase you a bottle of Marine Phytoplankton here www.7dayfitness.com/marine-phytoplankton-anti-aging-super-drops/. I have not found it in stores as of yet. (Hmmmm I wonder why!!!).
2. Upon rising after drinking a full glass of water, take two drops orally.
3. Then before you go to bed take two more drops orally.

Now remember. Wesley Virgin is not a doctor or a seasoned college student in any way! This is my personal experience on how I design the amazing life I live on a daily basis.

So many ask, Wesley, tell me more about this Acidic and Alkalinity deal. After years of trying stuff I discovered you do not have to go to medical school for 10 years to figure out how the body functions. Let me give you an example on how acidic and alkalinity works (By the way you want to be Alkaline).

If you take your trash out and leave it on your porch for weeks at a time and continue to pour more trash on top of the current trash, what happens? It starts to stink! The trash inside the bag starts to rot!! Then it starts to attract bugs, worms, insects and all type of disgusting creatures.

Well you know what? This is the exact same thing that happens within our bodies. After we trashed our bodies in our 20s and early 30s, you start to feel and see interesting things happen to your quality of life. By age 40, you will reap a return from your food investment of the past 30 years.

Investment?

Yes, investment... Your bad food investments that is... And your return is as follows: Cancer, heart disease, high blood pressure, diabetes and many more illnesses we still believe are genetically transferred from our parents.

I call BS!!

It is not genetics... it is lifestyle!! If your mom fed her family greasy foods, white bread and used Zatarans on every meal for the past 20 years, then yes, it is highly likely you will repeat the same generational curse. People are creatures of habit and I am going to bet you dollars to donuts that you are unconsciously repeating the same patterns of your parents or your childhood environment. But we call it genetics. No Sir and No Mam!! It's how you live!

You can break the generational curse now and ensure your family lives amazing and super healthy lives. So let me show you how to become a self-certified doctor by mastering Acidic and Alkalinity... Check out the video I created here that deep dives into the details of acidic and alkaline. www.7dayfitness.com/acidic-vs-alkaline/.

7

The Secret of Motivation

The only reason it is so difficult for you to stay motivated when working out is this: You do not know or have not written down your STANDARDS OF EXCELLENCE! Wes, what does standards of excellence have to do with losing weight? Let me tell you.

The only reason I am able to maintain and get consistent results from my body, is because I raise my standards daily! It is never the matter of ability; it is always a matter of motivation. I want you to think about the things in your life you do on autopilot. No motivation is necessary.

- Getting your hair done
- Getting your nails done
- Going to the barber shop
- Watching a football game
- Watching reality shows
- Going to work
- Brushing your teeth
- Drinking alcohol (Happy Hour!)
- Watching a movie
- Eating!!!

The above items are done unconsciously; they are done automatically which means you do not have to think about them. But I am going tell you this—there is some form of motivation in every item that was listed above.

I strive to not only show you how wonderful healthy living can be, but to share the information with everyone who honestly wants a healthier and happier life. We don't want to just look good; we also want to feel good as well!!!

Now what I would like to do is give you a few techniques that will work if you experience the issue of: working out for an entire week but losing your motivation on the following Monday. After a long day at the job, you just don't have the energy or drive to work-out.

So here is my personal ritual, which I use on a daily basis (I have only shared this with Superstars who are currently paying me 10k per month):

First thing is go to your computer and find an attractive picture of someone that you would like your body to look like. Go ahead and do it.

Then proceed to print at least 10 copies of this picture preferably using a color printer. Then with a blue marker write: "I have a body and physique just like _____+ (name of person)"

Then purchase some thumbtacks and place the pictures in the following areas:

1. Bathroom Mirror
2. Bedroom Ceiling
3. Bedroom left wall and right wall
4. Right under your TVs in all rooms
5. On your kitchen refrigerator
6. On your oven
7. On your counter where you place your bills and keys
8. On the front door so when you leave you can clearly see it

So at this point you might think I am bananas, but let me explain to you how the brain works. To keep it simple there is a part of our brain which accepts pictures which influences our behavior 90 times more than someone reminding us to workout.

Think of a person whose body you would like yours to resemble. And I want you to imagine having their physique, shredded abs, Michelle Obama sculpted arms, firm and toned Jennifer Lopez or Brazilian booty (ladies only) with an awesome pair of amazing legs that should never be covered with pants. And to top it off imagine yourself getting the compliments and the constant admiration as that person probably receives as well.

How does that make you feel? Good!!! After thinking like this for several minutes you will begin to see yourself as they are. You will begin to imagine how it feels to run your hands around your tastefully sculpted physique. You will hear the compliments from your co-workers every morning and receive random emails from admirers at your job wishing you a great morning. See I know that success builds confidence and when you experience a day like that, this will motivate you to get off your butt and do a 7-Minute routine (I will give you a good one that has changed lives in a later chapter).

But here is the problem that I have seen time and time again. Most of us are replaying the same unattractive sad picture over and over again in our minds. We tend to keep seeing ourselves as we **are** instead of seeing ourselves as **how we would like to be**! If you keep thinking about how fat, obese and unattractive you are, how can you expect to be motivated and excited to work-out? It's not going to happen, my friend.

You must start to create a body image that excites you. This is where what I call the ultimate resource, plays a huge part.

And it's called Faith. You must see your amazing body clearly in the invisible every single day!! You do this by engaging in what is called self-talk, where you speak to yourself and tell yourself how you would like to be instead of beating yourself up on how you are. Still skeptical? Then I have a question for you.

Why do you go to work?

"Well because I need to get paid, Wes!!"

Why do you need to get paid?

"Well. Because if I do not work, then I cannot pay my bills or take care of my family."

And how does that feel if you cannot do those things?

"It feels bad of course!!"

Right!! So the reason why most of us continually go to a job we abhor and freaking detest is because we are afraid of the illusion of what might happen if we leave or quit. Here are some of the reasons that are keeping you at the 8 to 5 grind!!!

I might get reprimanded if I don't go in. I might get fired. I want be able to pay my bills. I will lose all my benefits. Someone there might take my job. I will lose everything if I leave...

Even though you might have seen these things happen to other people or even yourself, it is an illusion because at the exact moment it hasn't happened. So we keep our butts warming a chair for 8 hours a day because we want to avoid the Pain of those things that might happen if we take an unplanned exodus.

This strategy takes me to my next tip. You might not

believe my next statement, but it is absolutely true. This is the driving force of why we do what we do. This is the reason why we don't work-out. This is the reason why we choose healthy or unhealthy meals. This is the reason why we drink, smoke and eat obsessively. Are you ready!?

We do more to avoid Pain than to gain Pleasure!! Say it with me slowly: *People do more to avoid Pain than to gain Pleasure.*

Let's be real here. The only reason why most of us are working out, starving ourselves and busting our butts in the gym, is because of some event (wedding, vacation, cruise or the "its summer time epidemic") initially we seek the pleasure that gets us started. Right?

But the only reason we fail to be consistent, is because we do more to avoid the Pain of working out (sweating, soreness or body discomfort) than to get the pleasure (the amazing beach body that will have the opposite sex drooling). But Let me bring this full circle and give you a real life example on how the Pain and Pleasure model works.

I have a buddy from high school that sent me a message on Facebook, and he told me he wanted me to help him lose 30 lbs. so he could be more active with his kids and be more physically appealing to his wife...

So I said sure. We are going to call him, Pookie. So I said Pookie let's do this!! I am ready! Just go to my site at www.7DayFitness.com and join the 7Day family, your life will never be the same...

Question: What do you think Pookie did?

Absolutely nothing!! I did not hear back from Pookie until 6 months later, when he wrote me another message but this one was quite devastating. He wrote, "Wes, I really need you help!" I replied, "You said that before, Pookie. What has changed?" He said: "Wes, I had a heart attack and the doctor told me if do not drop this weight, I won't be so lucky next time... And my wife is so stressed and worried about me it is affecting our marriage."

PAIN!!!

You can only guess what he did. He signed up for my program, purchased my advanced coaching program and he joined my 7Day Inner Circle group!!! By avoiding the pain of potentially dying and losing his wife, he lost 40 plus pounds in 45 days, runs and plays with his kiddos and his marriage is stronger than ever!

So, can you tell me why Pookie all of sudden chose to take action and went full force without any excuses or procrastination? Sure you do. Pookie wanted to avoid the PAIN of hurting his family, having another heart attack, dying, and losing his wife. All the potential pain kept him motivated, patient and persistent through his weight loss journey.

We do more to avoid Pain than to get Pleasure...

So this is what I would like you to do to reinforce the first strategy. Write down ten Pains that you would like to avoid, very emotional things that might bring tears to your eyes. If you do not take action TODAY and start to stick with a workout regimen, what will happen to you in the future?

I will give you a few:

1. You may become morbidly obese.

2. You could possibly be diagnosed with high blood pressure, diabetes or heart disease.

3. You will never be able to enjoy or keep up with your children at the park.

4. You could lose your marriage or significant other because your sex drive and sex endurance will decline.

5. You will always be the only person wearing a shirt to the pool or at the beach.

6. You will be forced to take insulin shots for the rest of your life

7. You will always lack confidence and self-esteem because of your appearance.

8. You will hate to look at yourself naked in the bathroom mirror, it will make you very sad and very depressed.

9. People will look at you in public, not because they are attracted to you, but because they are disgusted by you.

10. Your children will have to deal with the same rude and hurtful comments if something doesn't change.

I know that sounds harsh, but that is the PAIN which will motivate you, my friend. And I promise you if you use these easy and super simple strategies for the next 30 days, you will never exhaust your motivation! You will be eager to perfect your body!! Your friends and family will compliment you with love and genuine admiration. Men and women will notice you and almost fawn over you because you are transforming your body into a tastefully delicious piece of art.

I want you to know that I care about you. And I know how it feels not be comfortable in your skin. I know how it feels to be around a lot of people and wondering if someone is talking about you. I know how it feels not being able to wear the fun fitted clothes that show off your physique. I totally get it!!

But whatever pain you have felt in the past or maybe the

pain you are feeling right now, it is not valid because your past does not make your future. Stop driving your car looking over your shoulder at all the past failures. You will crash if you don't turn around and look straight ahead at the successes to come.

Even if I never get the chance to meet you, or train you at www.7Dayfitness.com, I am proud that you made it through this chapter. I encourage you to read it again and do the exercises listed in this book. The strategies in these chapters have changed many people's lives for the better. Start an amazing journey that will change the rest of your life. Get Fit With Passion.

8

Never Have to Buy another Weight Loss Product after Reading this Chapter

Long term weight loss is easy!! Yes, I said easy!! I mean, think about it...

- How do you keep your teeth white?
- How do you ensure you keep getting your weekly or bi-weekly paycheck?
- How do you keep your body clean?
- How do you increase the connection with your significant other?
- How do you ensure your children know you love them?
- How do you keep your sex life hot and steamy?

WE WORK AT IT DAILY!!! Duh!

Folks!! It is no secret. Anything you focus on or work on will expand. So the lack of doing some activity will create a **LACK OF RESULTS!**

<u>Say if you stopped doing the above items, here's what you will have to deal with:</u>

- Stale Breath
- You will have an awful body odor
- You will Lose Your Job
- You will be Divorced or Lonely
- Children will feel unloved and act out
- Your lover will leave you or sleep with your friend who is better in bed
- No long term weight loss
- No Happiness
- No Confidence
- No Joy
- No Sexy Body. Whew!!

To put it plainly, you must work on your temple daily. But I know what you are saying. It is not that easy Wes! Life demands, children, jobs, family!!! How can I possibly direct my focus?!

Do you really want to know? I want to challenge you, if

you are serious about directing your focus and killing the lethargic and sedentary behavior.

With conviction and expectation I want you to do this motivational exercise with me! When was the last time you went to a football or basketball game, concert, club, church, or watched some sporting event on TV?

What did you do when your team scored the winning point? How did you cheer when your favorite artist, like Beyonce and Jay Z, hit the stage? What did you do when you heard your favourite song play at your local club or pub? What do you do when the preacher starts whooping and hollering?

What is your reaction? You holler!! You Scream! You Cheer! You get filled with a significant amount of emotion and joy!

So today I would like you to cheer and scream! Are you ready? Ok, let's go!

I want you to Scream and Shout these 7 "New You" Affirmations!

1) I believe I have the power to create an amazing body.
2) I make the decision to run even when I feel all I can do is crawl.
3) I eliminate negative people who are not adding to my life or encouraging my goals.
4) I expect the best! Even when it appears that I'm getting the worst.
5) I decide to be a Freaking WINNER!! Because Winners Win and Losers Lose!

6)   I look around and see what everyone else is doing… And do the OPPOSITE!

7)   I am trusting in my creator, the universe, and myself, that I will SUCCEED in all things!

Ok how do you feel? I know it may feel a bit embarrassing or uncomfortable. Trust me, it was hard for me at first because I did not believe all those things were possible. But let me be the first to tell you, that it happened!! It really happened for me! Which is the reason why now it is time for me to share my story with you, and let you know that it is possible.

9

The Secret 7 Minute Workout
That Changes Lives

So in this chapter I would like to expose the real truth about exercise routines and the duration it takes to create the body you desire. First and foremost, everyone wants something different when they begin a workout regimen.

✓ Some of us want to be skinny.
✓ Some of us want to be lean and toned.
✓ Some of us want to get rid of cellulite.
✓ Some of us want to be ripped.
✓ Some of us want a body that is fit with curves.
✓ Some of us want the hourglass figure.
✓ And some of us want the abs that you can wash your underwear on!

The reason why so many people jump from program to program, trainer to trainer, gym to gym, nutritionist to nutritionist, DVD to DVD is because they do not have a clear picture of what they would like their body to be.

Think about it for a second. As soon as you watch that late night fitness infomercial or see that amazing guy or gal with that sexy ass delicious body, what do you tell yourself?

Well you say, "You know. I need to work out."

"My mind is made up, I am going to get my butt in the gym tonight..."

"I want my body to look like that!"

But after the first week or within the first 30 days, what tends to happen? Well you quit, but not without giving yourself justifiable reasons for why you quit.

Do any of these excuses sound familiar:

- Well, I just do not have the time.
- The routines are too hard for me.
- The doctor says I cannot do these types of workouts.
- My trainer is mean to me!
- My back and joints are killing me after these routines, not for me.
- I have kids and I do not have the time.
- I am not seeing any results after the first week so obviously this program doesn't work.
- For some reason I am gaining weight instead of losing it, not for me.
- I have to go church on the evenings that I am scheduled to go to the gym, Darn!!

Side note: You will be surprised at the number of people that have used God or going to church as an excuse of not being able to commit to a workout. God bless them all. LOL

These types of excuses and procrastinations go on for months, even years! But remember the title of this book. Lose fat and weight without the struggle. So let's get back to what you want instead of what you don't want!!

<u>FOCUS</u>

I use the word focus, why? Because most of us focus on what we do not want. We focus on the pain of working out. We focus on our huge belly when getting out of the shower butt naked. We focus on the pain of our legs, bones, joints and back. We focus on the negative people that tell us that the workout is not working. We focus on the long and arduous time it will take us to create the body we desire

Quite frankly…We focus on everything that makes us feel BAD!! WHY? Because we have been conditioned to feel this way. Read closely… Stay with me here… I am going to bring this full circle in a second.

Most of us, myself included, were told NO and were consistently reminded of our limitations during our early adolescent years.

I remember these statements when I was at home.

- ❖ No you can't go outside
- ❖ No you can't go over to your friend's house
- ❖ No you can't get name brand shoes or clothes
- ❖ No you cannot get a cookie out of the cookie jar
- ❖ No we can't afford that
- ❖ No, money does not grow on trees
- ❖ No you can't do that
- ❖ No you are not big or tall enough to do that
- ❖ No don't touch that
- ❖ No do not go over there

No No No No…

Now in all fairness, some of these no's are important to keep us safe and out of harm's way. But when all a child hears is what he or she cannot do, repeatedly, he or she grows up to believe life is full of limitations. He or she starts to live with what I call an "I Can't Lifestyle" instead of an "I Can Lifestyle."

Unfortunately we are conditioned to fail in life... We are told and constantly reminded about our limitations. And let me make this statement, this is through no fault of our parents. They are teaching their children what has been taught to them.

So yes, people are monkeys!!! We do what other people do. We buy what other people buy. We go to places where other people go. We do what other people tell us to do. We shop where other people tell us to shop. We even purchase fitness programs that other people tell us to purchase.

Still don't believe me... Let me give you an example. It's a bit off topic, but I think it will help you understand things better.

Most families today have an 8 to 5 job. Have at least 1 or 2 cars. Have a couple of kiddos... Live in an apartment, or a house. Save what money they can. Go out on the weekend to have fun with friends and family... And plan vacations no more than 3 times a year.

Sounds like most of us, right? Now no offense, but when this type of person is presented with a business opportunity which requires them to quit their job, he or she immediately feels the fear of loss, like:

- "How will I pay my bills while I build this business?"
- "How can I support me and my family if I don't have steady income coming in?"

- "The business is a risk and my job is a guarantee!"

They get the "No Feeling," basically. They feel a new business opportunity, which can replace their current day-to-day grind job, is a risk!!

But on the other hand, you have another family which has a business. That doesn't need to work an 8 to 5 job. Has 4 cars in 4 different countries around the world. Has several homes and condos around the world. And they don't plan for vacations. No, no, no... They TAKE vacations! Whenever they feel like it. And the second family feels that family no. 1 (the one that works an 8 to 5 job) has more risk than they do.

How? Wes, you are not making sense here.

Well, read closely...

The second family has a business, which means they have thousands of customers who they provide service for around the world. Basically the 2nd family is getting checks and transactions from thousands of people while the first family is only getting one check from that one job. So if the first family loses the job, they are screwed. They lose the house, the car, the wife and most of all, they lose stability and happiness. But if the second family loses one customer or even several, their lifestyle doesn't change much at all.

So what is the point here?

Everyone has a very unique perception in life. Perception is one's current reality! For most of us who hear the word risk, we think of the Pain that we would get from losing something if the situation doesn't work out. Many will focus solely, and create illusions on, the "Bad" and how much worse it may become if it doesn't work out...

Others when they take risk, they see opportunity and the possibility of gain. They focus on the good and what good can become of the risk they are taking. Same person but completely different mindset!

So what I would like you to do right now, while you are reading this book, is to focus on what you want. Take a gander at what I call my "Focus Declarations." No matter the events or circumstances in my life, this is what I concentrate my attention on.

I think about the millions of people who will not only get great value from this book, but how it will transform their lives.

I focus on how smart and super intelligent my kiddos are, and how they are getting stronger and smarter every day.

I focus on how hot, ripped and delicious my body will become after dedicating a few minutes a day towards it.

I focus on the gratitude and compliments of others who have benefited from my hard work.

I focus on having an abundance of money, love, respect, gratitude and enjoyment that exponentially increases every single day of my life.

I focus on my amazing family who supports my efforts and gives me an abundance of love.

I focus on the beautiful houses and the exotic cars and yachts that I am purchasing every 3 months.

I am focusing on the media appearance on shows like Oprah Life Class, Dr. Phil, and Dr. Oz, inspiring millions of people to be at their best.

I am focusing on giving my children 10 times the amount of love and letting them know how great and how beautiful they are.

I focus on expanding the energy, power and vitality that my God has given me at birth.

I am sorry for being long winded. ;) But I focus and I want a lot. And a man or woman gets what he or she thinks about most of the time. You might say: "Well Wesley, you have that type of life already. I am still trying to get there..."

Let me be transparent with you here. Most of those things I listed hasn't even taken place yet. You might say, Well Wes I cannot say something I don't believe... RIGHT?

Why not!!! Yes you can!!

Most of us are in pain, we struggle, we hurt, we are depressed, we are down, emotionally scarred, confused, beat up, and the list goes on... And guess what, you create the pain, you create struggle, and you create the feeling of depression... You are 100 percent responsible for all the headache, hurt and discomfort in your life...

Because we solely focus on and feel that bad emotion of a situations or events in our life. It is always those damn "What If" statements.

- *What if it doesn't work?*

- *What if I get hurt?*
- *What if I waste my money?*
- *What if I waste my time?*
- *What if she rejects me?*
- *What if I fail?*
- *What if it doesn't come through?*

When you use this type of disempowering language, you create using your words from your mouth. Fear, lack, and disbelief!!! But let me show you how to reverse this process today, yes today!!!

Hey! By changing something simple as your focus, and the words that are spoken out of your mouth, you can drastically change your body, relationships, money and every aspect of your life so you can feel the abundance and the juice of life. And it taste amazing!!

So, before I give you the short 7-minute workout that has worked for tens of thousands of people who have joined me and became a superstar at www.7DayFitness.com, let me give you the first technique you need to do before you begin. I would like you do write out your focus list...

But first a question: When you read my focus list, how did you feel? Did you smile, were you inspired, did you want some of that stuff as well? I hope so...

Now in the 10 blanks below I would like you to write 10 things that you like to get once you are in the body you desire. Now, this is personal stuff. I want you to be selfish, vain, outrageous and just plain silly with these focus declarations. Each statement should make you smile or activate that amazing emotion called love...

You should put these statements on your iPhone, write them on your bathroom mirror, post them on your wall, write them on your Facebook wall everyday (tagging me of course at 7DayFitness), Instagram them and watch how your friends and other people validate you and give you energy towards your focus declarations...

1.
2.
3.
4.
5.
6.
7.
8.
9.
10.

How do I know this works?

Well let me show you. Take a second and browse www.facebook.com/7DayFitness. Friend or follow me and scroll thru my wall and pay attention to my post very closely. I only post those things that are good and I only post those things that helped other people as well. I do not post anything negative or anything that will give a person a feeling of hurt or pain. I encourage people like yourself to be an example that it is possible to become better than your best.

So let me give you some homework for the next 30 days.

1. After following me or friending me on Facebook…
2. Post something encouraging every day on your wall or my wall and tag Wesley Virgin on each post.

3. Do the below 7-minute workout and let me know every day that you finished your workout.
4. Read your Focus Declarations every single day. 7 Days!
5. I will _Like_ or respond to your post so you know someone is watching and paying attention to ya.
6. Everyday tell someone that you love them. Anyone!!!!
7. Every morning take 15 seconds to be grateful of what you have and be grateful of those things to come.
8. Do the other affirmations listed in the previous chapters of this book.

These 7 days will change your body but most importantly it will change your perception of life. For you will only focus on the Good in life. You will focus on the love and joy!

Ok, let's get to the good stuff or should I say the great stuff. The 7-minute simple workout below will change your life! You are going to complete 7 different exercises targeting every muscle around your body in a 7-minute timeframe.

It doesn't matter how simple you think the below workout is, this is what I did for several years to build foundation. And get this. I still do the same routines today in the comfort of my living room or children's room.

Most of us forget about the basics, you know, the simple stuff. But if you insist on using weights and heavy equipment, I call this the "Bigger is Quicker and Better" mentality. You will end up hurt and gain more weight because you will soon become sedentary or even immobilized.

Ok if you see below there is a workout for women and then a workout for men. Women first, of course.

7-Minute Women Daily Workout Routine

Mon – Saturday
(Sunday is a Rest Day)

Jump Rope, 28 Jumps
Mountain Climber, 28 Reps
Pushups, 28 Reps (knee pushups are fine)
Sit-ups with the legs up, 28 Reps
Overhead hand claps, 28 Reps
Supiners, 28 Reps
Bouncy Wouncies (Visit www.7DayFitness.com/blog to see an example)

Completion Time: _____ Goal Time: 7 Minutes

If you visit www.7DayFitness.com and go to my blog, you will see a list of home workouts to model the correct form.

Do the above workout 1 time per day within a 7-minute timeframe. If it takes you longer than 7 minutes then that is fine, but you ultimately want to get up to 7 minutes. Always make sure to notate your time every day on a piece of paper! This will give you the opportunity to measure yourself.

Ok gents, here is your 7-minute routine for the next week.

Jump Rope, 28 Jumps
Mountain Climber, 28 Reps
Manly Pushups, 28 Reps
Sit-ups with the legs up, 28 Reps
Overhead hand claps, 28 Reps
Supiners 28 Reps
Bouncy Wouncies(Visit www.7DayFitness.com/blog to see an example)

If you visit www.7DayFitness.com and go to my blog, you will see a list of home workouts to model the correct form.

Do the above workout 1 time per day within a 7-minute timeframe. If it takes you longer than 7 minutes then that is fine, but you ultimately want to get up to 7 minutes. Always make sure to notate your time every day on a piece of paper!

For a complete uncut experience with MVT Wesley Virgin, please come visit me here at www.7DayFitness.com.

10

In Conclusion:
Bringing It All Together

Well you have approached the end of my book and I would like to ask you a question. This is the question you should ask yourself whenever you hear or read great information that can literally change your life.

This is the question that makes you feel a certain way. You know what I mean?

- This is the same feeling you feel when you leave church on Sundays all fired up ready to live a better life.

- This is the same feeling you feel when you leave your morning sales meeting all ready to conquer the world to provide for your family.

- This is the same feeling you feel after a money or business opportunity meeting, hearing all the success stories which make you feel that you too can have a piece of the American dream.

- This is the same feeling you get when you meet that man or woman that makes you smile privately at your desk for no apparent reason.

- This is the same feeling when your baby graduates and walks across that stage proud and excited.

So you may ask, what is the question, Wes? What is the question that will determine my success or my failure after I put this book down? What happens tomorrow when I have to get up in the morning, go to work, pay the bills, take the kids to school, deal with my silly co-workers and all the other unforeseen issues of life?

The question is this:
WHAT ARE YOU GOING TO DO ABOUT IT?

Tell me!! What are you going to do now? TODAY! Are you going to get super motivated and inspired, ready to conquer your body and the world?

After you finish this book you may say:

- I am going to make some changes now!! I am going to find a fitness program that I can stick with.

- I am going to be more grateful and show others genuine approbation every day! I am going to stop nagging at my spouse and show them love even when I feel I am not being loved.

- I am going to stop criticizing others when they share ideas with me and just encourage them and wish them the best!

- I am going to tell my children I love them and hold them close for at least 60 seconds every day, so they will never need to seek love outside of the family.

- I am going to raise my standards daily and become an excellent human being!

- I am going to learn to appreciate and receive compliments and gifts without feeling guilty of not being worthy!

- I am going to affirm that I am slim, hot, sexy and trim!

- I am going to put down the foods that will eventually make my life a living HELL, and replenish my body with superfoods so I can have energy and watch my child or grand-baby walk across the graduation stage one day!

Question for ya...

➢ How many books have you read that has inspired you and even provoked you to do better in life?

➢ How many audio programs have you listened to that told you things that you already knew, but failed to execute?

➢ How many hotel seminars, fitness classes and conference talks have you attended, but still failed to give 100%?

➢ How many people in your life have showed you unconditional love, but you were not able to accept it!

➢ How many hours have you searched the web in the wee hours of the night, trying to find a solution for your weight loss, money, relationship, or life situation?

➢ How many magazines do you read only to feel depressed because you see men and women that have bodies that you believe you could never have?

➢ How many times are you going to say?
  - *It's almost summer time, time to lose weight*
  - *It's a New Year! I am going to make some changes this*

year!

- *I am going on vacation so I need to lose 10 to 30 pounds FAST!!*
- *I am getting married! Yah!! I need to lose this weight to get into this dress!*
- *I am going to a wedding!! I need to lose this weight to get into this dress!*

We all had periods in our life where we have thought like this, including myself, but I have made a daily conscious choice to raise my standards every single day! If you decide to follow me, be trained by me or just watch how I live for the next 20 (or even 200!) years, you will see a man who has dedicated his life to excellence.

I am not sure if I will ever become this EXCELLENT PERSON that I feel I am destined to become, but I will continue to write books, create audio programs, make workout videos, post words of inspiration on Facebook/Twitter but most of all serve people like yourself, to let you know that IT IS POSSIBLE!!!!

✓ It is possible to live a happy life every single day of your life.

✓ It is possible to have children that adore you without belts and yelling at them!

✓ It is possible to be sexy, fit and have an amazing body that others admire!

✓ It is possible to have a bank account that has more money than you could ever spend or give!

✓ It is possible to leave a job you hate and find a job and

start a business that pays you well and makes you happy.

✓ It is possible to tip waiters and waitresses 100 - 300% just because that is the type of person you are!

✓ It is possible to vacation around the world every month to some exotic island with your family!

✓ It is possible to EXCEL easily in a world that appears to be so cynical and negative!

✓ It is possible to find the man or woman of your dreams who will make you happy and love you every second of the day!

✓ It is possible to tell that person in your life, you have had it! And attract the person who will love you for you!

✓ It is possible to tell yourself you are awesome even when it feels you are not!

✓ It is possible to tell yourself, while looking in the mirror, that you Love Yourself!! Even if it feels strange!

So... WHAT ARE YOU GOING TO DO ABOUT IT? Is this the time in your life when your back is against the wall? When you feel worried because you do not know where to start?

o Maybe you want to know if you are making the right decision.
o Maybe you would like to know how your life is going to play out.
o Maybe you want to know if you are on the right path that GOD has laid out for you.

- o Maybe you are afraid that you might waste time if you make the wrong decision.
- o Maybe you have been hurt so many times that you feel trying again would be silly and stupid!
- o Maybe you think it is too late to try to fix your marriage, your body or your life.
- o Maybe it is too late to go back to school.
- o Or maybe it is too late to tell that person you are sorry.
- o Or maybe it is too late to start dreaming again.
- o Or maybe you are that person who is afraid of sharing things, because people may judge you on the things you have done in the past.

Hey!! I have overcome plenty and more!! And like I said in the beginning of this book, I am going to be very transparent and take the first step for you and share some of the things from my past.

- ❖ I have filed bankruptcy before.
- ❖ I have been to jail numerous times for silly traffic tickets.
- ❖ I have wrecked a car that almost cost me and a friend's life.
- ❖ I used to pay for gas only using ash tray change.
- ❖ My self-esteem was incredibly low while in my 20s… No one knew.
- ❖ I have been evicted out of many apartments.
- ❖ I have had broken leases.
- ❖ My credit was super jacked up. A 500 credit score!
- ❖ I used to sleep on floors because I could not get an apartment.
- ❖ I used to ride the bus for 4 hours a day only to make 10 bucks an hour.
- ❖ I have been fired more times than a little.
- ❖ I have never had a stable job for more than two years.
- ❖ I used to burn candles because I couldn't pay my light bill.

- ❖ I used to illegally turn the water back on outside when the city would turn it off for non-payment.
- ❖ I used to write bad checks and get the cash back because I didn't have any food to eat.
- ❖ I used to sleep in my car when my ex threatened to call the police on me.
- ❖ I used to hide my vehicles from the bank but they stilled repoed it! LOL.
- ❖ I have started many businesses and over 90 percent of them failed!
- ❖ I lived in a family that never said the words I LOVE YOU!

So I say again!! WHAT ARE YOU GOING TO DO ABOUT IT? See, I just aired my dirty laundry publicly, but so what!! Every issue and incident above has created the person you see today. So now the ball is in your court, my fellow Superstar.

Yes, you can make excuses and you can tell me all the reasons why you can't do something, but I challenge you.

I challenge you this... After you tell me all the reasons of why your situation is different, how I don't understand what's going on in your life and you might say, "Wes if you just knew what I was going through, then you would understand."

I challenge you to ask yourself this one question, before I end this book and get ready to experience my next luxurious beach adventure.

Tell me, why you CAN...That simple!! Just remove the '**t** and tell me why you CAN!

So Where To Go From Here?

So where to go from here?

I have been in the fitness industry for quite awhile now, about 10 years, and to be honest, I have learned new and very innovative techniques to get and maintain the body I have today. I mean who wants to work harder if they don't have to...

So I spent 2 years reviewing over 500 online programs, books and pdf's; and out of 500, only 3 of them made the cut...

So I am sure you have heard about Mike Geary. I actually met this young man in Vegas... He is one of the most knowledgeable guys I have ever met about the complexities of the stomach muscle I call the poochie pooch. LOL...

I learned a lot from reading his eBook and actually use many of his secrets today. Truth about abs is probably one of the best eBooks about abs and nutrition you will ever buy!!

You can get it at: www.7dayfitness.com/truthaboutabs

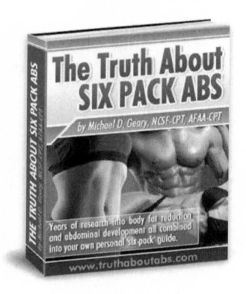

This book literally changed my life! This is one of the most amazing and cheapest books I have ever purchased!

It literally gave me a different perspective not just on my body but on life in general. After reading this book, My body went to a new an amazing level, my energy and confidence soared and believe it or not my finances tripled in 12 months.

This book really compliments the 7DayFitness Blueprint and it is dirt cheap.

My great friend Tyler is one of the coolest guys you will ever meet! He is a family man like myself and in his book the 27 Transformational Habits, he shares the core rituals you can do to really become an amazing person, physically, emotionally and spiritually.

You can get it at:  www.7dayfitness.com/27habits

And last, I am going to tell you a little secret this program called Old School New Body. You know at times when you think you know everything about a certain subject? You know when you think you are the freaking expert! Then you meet someone who knows 100 times more than you and better yet is getting results much faster?

Well let me introduce you to my friend John Rowley! As you know I am quickly approaching the age of 40 and he being over 50 John has enlightened me. In the Old School New Body ebook he shares information that blew my mind. To be honest I currently use his program along with my 7DayFitness System to keep lean and beach ready on autopilot.

You can check out his program below but for outstanding results I would use my system as a starter because it only uses your body weight and check out Old School New Body because he implements a few weights to enhance definition.

You can get it at: www.7dayfitness.com/oldschoolnewbody

Much Love,
Your Trainer and Friend,

Wesley Virgin IV
Master Virtual Trainer
Master Motivator

World Authority on Health and Fitness
Life Expert

From the Author

Check out my blog for Updates and interesting info.

Author Blog – http://www.7dayfitness.com

If you enjoyed any of my books then please share the love and click LIKE on my books in Amazon.

If you write me a review and send me an email I will send you a free book, or many.
(Just know that these emails are filtered by my publisher.)

Good news is always welcome.

One Last Thing, For Kindle Readers...

When you turn the page, Kindle will give you the opportunity to rate this book and share your thoughts on Facebook and Twitter. If you enjoyed my writings, would you please take a few seconds to let your friends know about it? Because... when they enjoy they will be grateful to you and so will I.

Thank You!

Wesley Virgin
wesley_virgin@awesomeauthors.org

About the Author

Wesley Virgin simply cannot be described nor defined. Instead, he should be experienced. The remarkable combination of his personal style and his message does something to people that cannot be captured in a text description. The power that is behind his extraordinary effect on people is not found just in what he enables them to learn, but in what he makes them feel. Time spent with Wesley Virgin, whether at a live seminar or through his audio and video programs, is an indescribable emotional journey that will expand your self-confidence, rekindle your determination to succeed and enrich your attitude – further intensifying your ambition to alter your life for the better.

Wesley Virgin is the creator of RSDP, the revolutionary mental and physical fitness system that will help millions of people around the world get in shape and and not focus on the supposed painful process!

With a desire and definiteness of purpose to positively affect the lives of over 100 million people personally, spiritually, physically, financially, Wesley's mentor ship, training and motivation increasingly help others open their eyes to life's possibilities, GET FIT WITH PASSION.

Made in the USA
San Bernardino, CA
17 April 2017